PRAIRIE SCHOONER BOOK PRIZE IN POETRY ⋮ EDITOR: HILDA RAZ

Ceiling of Sticks

Shane Book

UNIVERSITY OF NEBRASKA PRESS : LINCOLN AND LONDON

FUNDED BY:

 Canada Council   Conseil des Arts
for the Arts   du Canada

ONTARIO ARTS COUNCIL
CONSEIL DES ARTS DE L'ONTARIO

Library of Congress Cataloging-in-
Publication Data
Book, Shane.
Ceiling of sticks / Shane Book.
p.   cm.
ISBN 978-0-8032-1558-0
(pbk. : alk. paper)
I. Title.
PS3602.O65745C45   2010
811'.6—dc22
2010001291

Set in Bulmer by Bob Reitz.
Designed by Nathan Putens.

For my mother, my father, and my sister

Contents

Acknowledgments

Acknowledgment is made to the following magazines and anthologies, both online and in print, in which some of the poems in this book previously appeared (sometimes in slightly different form):

IX Cave Canem Anthology 2004: "Homecoming"
Black Nature: Four Centuries of African American Nature Poetry: "The Lost Conquistador"
Bluesprint: Black British Columbian Literature and Orature: "The Lost Conquistador" originally published as "Insect from the Lost Conquistador series" and "Offering"
Breathing Fire 2: Canada's New Poets: "Offering" and "Litost: A Style Manual"
Cave Canem V 2000 Anthology: "Offering"
Cimarron Review: "Litost: A Style Manual"
The Cortland Review: "Uganda, 1997"
Event: "Blind Woman of Gondan"
www.fishousepoems.org: "The One" and "Stark Room"
From the Fishouse: An Anthology of Poems: "The One" and "Stark Room"
Grain: "The Beach", originally published as "Belly Down"
Hammer and Tongs: A Smoking Lung Anthology: "Dust"
The Iowa Review: "Homecoming"
The Malahat Review: "Dust" and "Santa Cruz"
Phatitude: "Offering"
PN Review: "Mistakes"
The Poetry Center's Rella Lossy Poetry Award Anthology: "Dust," and "Offering
Revival: An Anthology of Black Canadian Writing: "The One"
Ryga: "The Market," "My People," "Stop," and "To a Curl of Water"

Witness: "Photograph of Religious Sacrifice, Tarahumara, Mexico, 1984," "The One"
Vintage 1999: "Offering"

"The One," "Photograph of Religious Sacrifice, Tarahumara, Mexico, 1984," "Uganda, 1997," "Blind Woman of Gondan," "My People," and "Stop" were inspired by Sebastião Salgado's photographs.

This work was made possible by the support of the Breadloaf Writers' Conference, The Canada Council for the Arts, the Cave Canem Foundation, the Chalmers Arts Fellowship, the Ford Foundation, the Jerome Foundation, The MacDowell Colony, the Naropa University Summer Writing Program, *The New York Times* Foundation, New York University, the Ontario Arts Council, the Poetry Center and American Poetry Archives, Randolph College, the Rella Lossy Endowment, Instituto Sacatar Brazil, Stanford University, The University of Iowa, The University of Victoria, and the Wallace Stegner Fellowship.

I owe a debt of gratitude to many people for encouragement and critical feedback during the writing of this book, including Eavan Boland, Joan Brennan, Xochiquetzal Candelaria, Lorna Crozier, Toi Derricotte, W. S. Di Piero, Camille Dungy, Cornelius Eady, Ken Fields, Jim Galvin, Melissa Hammerle, Adrian Harewood, Tyrone Geronimo Johnson, Patrick Lane, David Lau, Mark Levine, Philip Levine, and Gregory Pardlo. Thank you.

CEILING OF STICKS

CEILING OF STICKS

Litost: A Style Manual

I remember reading somewhere
of a Czech word, *litost,*
                that means too much
to be translated properly —
a wild mixture of sorrow, regret, empathy
                        an inexhaustible longing.
At one time I would have said
it sounded like all the things
                we might take from this life
distilled to the smallest salt crystal
                    on a blade of grass.
Or the worst possible sadness.

I wonder about that now
                  how something can be possible
yet infinite
and all I can think of are the countless cracks
                      in the pad of a dog's paw
raised in mid-stride,
                body rigid with instinct.
Perhaps in this way instinct is a precursor to form
so that it is not darkness
                but instinct that hems in
the tree's silhouette
on a ragged grass patch in Washington Square park
                    in the strange light of late afternoon . . .

And sadness?

Sometimes those old days seem so far away,
with their despair and other stories.

One night a friend called
said he'd just gotten back from an all night drive
to try to save his marriage.

The previous evening
                          walking past the Budget Car Rental Office
on Douglas Street
                he'd stopped in mid-stride,
wheeled and gone in.
Minutes later he came out driving
what was left on the lot:
                        a bright red cargo van
for the twelve hours north on mountain roads.

It didn't matter that when he showed up at his old door
his wife would be leaving for work
                            a strange look on her face,
the question, *What are you doing here?*
ringing out across the driveway
                    in the clean morning air.

All I could do was smile and point at the van,
                        he told me, voice cracking,
say, Look honey, it's red.

The past is a loan shark. It lends to anyone.
And you can never pay it back.

That word *litost* can also mean too little
to be translated correctly —
a thumbprint as singular as the shade of green
on a grass blade
                    a meaning as precise as the tools used by carvers
who make the delicate figurines
I once saw in an African Art shop window:
                                                    slender, dark wood,
teardrop shaped heads,
            bodies long to the ground
            without legs.

Holes had been carved through the heads.
An index card labeled them "Shadows,"
a name which —
        perhaps because I associate shadows
        in some vital way with the soul
        and imagine the soul living somewhere
        above the shoulders
                            — made no sense to me.

In parts of the world
                    when a loved one dies
they eat the brain
                    to stop the soul from returning.

Or is it to keep it close?

Another friend had a different solution —
he locked himself in his apartment,
                                cigarettes, a case of gin.
When finally he opened the door there was nothing left:
    mirror, arm chair, bicycle,
                        plates, stereo, potted plant,
        sacred heart painting —
all smashed in the alley below his window.
He'd shaved a strip of hair
                        down the middle of his chest
was sitting on a carpet of glass
                        talking on the phone.
A hand covered in cigarette burns
shielded the receiver as he looked up at us.
                                It was four a.m.
Keep it down guys, he said, *I'm talking with mother.*

I don't know what to call those wooden figures,
the name for what's left behind
                        after body, soul, after it all.

And I don't want to.

Something about the past
makes me want to lathe it down to perfection,
                        to nothing,
                        the finest wood dust . . .

6

The One

The enormous head and huge
bulbed knees, elongated
hands and feet, don't fit
with the filed down chest, limbs
of kindling, yet this is one
whole boy, suspended
in a cloth harness hooked
to what looks like a clock
stuck at three fifteen.
Closer, you can see it is
not a clock but a scale,
the kind you find in any North
American grocery,
but of course this is not
North America, this is
the Sahel famine, this
is Mali in 1985, where a boy
waiting for his rations
to be adjusted
must be weighed. At once
his face relays one and many
things: he could be crying out,
he could be grinning,
he could be frightened
or tired, he could believe
he is suspended in unending
dream. What starvation started
gravity refines as the boy

reclines, the hunger having
crumpled his neck, his face
staring up at the ceiling
of sticks which like most ceilings
anywhere in this world is blank.

Homecoming

Beside me a woman moves her lips
and I wonder if she's praying.
With his stunted machine
gun the checkpoint soldier waves
us down, stilling the drum and creak
of the *tro-tro* bus. In front of me
tightly strapped to a woman in bright
aqua homecoming cloth, a baby
stops gurgling, lays his head
down on her brown back,
closes his eyes. We file out into
a heat and red dust field.
A guardhouse, thin and shaky
like the soldiers, crumbling mud
walls, tin roof half ripped open
like a can of smoked oysters.
From somewhere, more guards
appear, more guns with taped-on
crescent-shaped magazines.
The one who waved us in walks
down the line, stopping at a watch,
shirt collar, face, as though
inspecting troops in the Independence
Day parade. Reeking of palm
wine, he sways and his dented
gun sways. Beside me a woman
moves her lips and I wonder
if she's praying. Someone's got
enough of what the soldiers want

and what is it. From her cloth bag
I smell pepper-smoke, dried fish.
The noon sun hits. Who among us
won't get back on the bus?
Peering at a child's sandals, the soldier
leans over too far, hitting
the red dirt hard. We don't say
anything. Another soldier shouts
and points at the fallen man
and the soldiers all laugh.
The one on the ground curses,
leans heavily on his gun
like a field hockey player getting
back on his feet. But he's
not a hockey player.
And that's when it starts.

The Lost Conquistador

A breeze beginning. Black, unshining flake
in shifting screens — these chopped in trees,
continually, then scattered loose,
no, not loose (note the small dance) then
shattered with their tethers hidden
still somehow attached — the flake
grounded now
　　　now moving (A beetle. A flying ant. A beetle.) along the sand path
among pieces of light and
in sudden wind:
　　　the glance in grass
the glance in swung around
　　　　　darkness
a dance of particulates, then a shifting
(bird wings beating water)
a coalescing . . .
　　　　　Refocus:
beetle at the green edge
(have I seen anything?)
　　　others no doubt
down there. Fidelity.
In extreme. In
the green wires sprung
from earth to meet his legs
the stutter
in each blade, the return
and there

the dirt's near invisible throwing
moves the glance
past tiny piled stones (little basilicas)
pinning what
slew, what shut motive
beneath them,
bulking some unseeable gathering, impossible to —
and what besides sand — the thinnest particulars — builds itself
impregnable grammar . . .

The beetle is not a messenger. I can see that.
He grows into things.
        The light around him. For example.

Is the fuse point of his leaving.
Is the clawing in the center.
Claimed by anything?
The focus.
    Is it claimed?: (Twig as bridge,
                    leaf shard as scrap of night)

And after the sunlight killings of small scenes,
the graying out.
And whose idea of a place in the vibrant guttural repose of an antlered
    thing . . .

Step
around to the green now
of where he might be
going.
Everything to
not lay a hand in his path.
Everything to

not smooth it over.
(What shall I do for my birthday?)
It might be
he stops
in patterns of sunlight
        a half step farther out,
it might be some loosening . . .

Lapse.
Location.
Lapse.

Comes now,
    burnished,
            a perfect translation of — a hiving out
of air
some small tar
intensity.
    Comes,
irreducible pinprick
        choosing through
                delicate green steeples.
Serious selector,
        how to distinguish (how to hurt)
A breeze beginning.
I lie on my side among the (watch now)
                phalanx guards of green,
            the bare
rigor of a broad mind in its plainness
its refusal to look (how to hurt)
the smile of light
on the shell,
        discrimination of the oblivious dark little hum

ground somehow
in the middle of a long light —
all the others (how to dream) — tendrils
frail legs
supporting
one thing,
    (how to damage)

now a breath hole

now a small turning

now a tiny reddish light

        stopped

now a clinging eye —

Photograph of Religious Sacrifice, Tarahumara, Mexico, 1984

Though blurred in the background, the first thing
you notice is the small white teeth, bared
in a smile, if that is the word, if goats can smile.
The boy in the foreground does not smile,
lips pressed hard together, nose slightly flared
as though he's just exerted himself.
Pulled up by a rope, one of the goat's hooves
hangs limp at the wrist, if that is the word,
if goats can have wrists. The goat skinned
from the neck down. The boy's hair, a helmet
of freshly shorn black bristles. The goat's neck
and the long bump of vein and switching sinew
of the neck and the neck stretched.
A shadow across the boy's eyes, the first
hairs of a mustache and the tiny pock mark
scars on his boy cheeks. The goat's long
bushy white beard. Something unseen pins
the head up high so the goat seems to teeter on
unseen hooves. Their eyes are open but not watching,
exactly, boy and goat poised, as if to say to some god
looming in the lens, *Is this what you want.*

Santa Cruz

The book on my lap is open to Aristotle's line about hallucinogenic cult members having to learn nothing
but experience something *and* be in a certain condition.
I'm listening to Chopin, watching Black Entertainment Television in my robe when the bikini
clad cow in the ice cream ad just slides onto the screen without a thought
and in a magazine beside me Wallace Stevens has a poor dumb Negress getting filled with hotness. "Fuck you,"
is too easy. Someone go get Jay-Z, he'll open a can

of chipotle whup ass on someone. I zap the TV. I can
just make out the clock: Four-ten. The fridge is cold and full of nothing
but nopales. On Front Street I duck into that pie place where you
can get a thick green tea. At LOGOS bookstore there's a mint condition
Atmosphere Conditions and an old book on the new thoughts
in physics to help my slurping. Some people apparently think atoms, bikinis,

even clouds are mostly space and the flesh of all things is that of thinking. "Bikinis" —
the word, always lacked a certain gravitas, no wonder! But can
all these dread locked blondes, strolling suits, Hare Krishna yelps, be thoughts?
I've got gas. Phew, no queue at the post office. There's nothing
worse than being stuck in line and breaking wind. I mail two gifts. It seems one condition
of Malcolm X getting on a stamp was he be painted to look like your

Boy Scout troop leader. Back on the street, the newspaper box — you
couldn't dream this: a war on and the front page with a picture of a bikini-
clad chimp. I keep walking. Past the palest harpist in the world whose voice is in no condition
for proving day in and out that Puff The Magic Dragon can
be varied ad infinitum, and the man with the sheer white hair who says nothing
and his tiny cardboard sign reading: Can't Sing, Can't Dance, Even Nice Thoughts

Help, and the gaggle of middle-aged bikers harboring thoughts
no doubt of running amok on the Starbucks patio and you
just know their cigarettes are making those two girls — who want nothing
other than to sip their lattes this finest sunny day in their cleanest, whitest bikini
tops — sick. It is striking me that the smell of smoke is so rare anymore I can't
recall the last time — when I step into a blast of sweet apple conditioner,

nearly kissing the puffed hair of a beautiful woman on a shiny cell. Conditioning
swivels my head, but she makes the streets, the crowds lighter. Graeme died. I thought
he committed suicide, it was March but it might have been October, can
one really tell the difference between spring and fall day lilts? The ATM spits you
some cash. Dodge a smiling man in a pink unitard beneath his foil umbrella, bikinied
sidewalk sale mannequins, the remains of a blue bike chained to nothing.

Where something you can't remember used to be, stoves are being re-conditioned.
At least nothing's harmed the dancing frog mural. Is a dissolving place the same as a last thought?
There is a feeling in my chest, an inescapable weather on an atoll called Bikini.

Stark Room

In a stark room I knelt and reeling, felt the wooden floor.
Against losing I was leaning, praying you'd left behind
a long hair in the brine. Soft animal gloves protected my sores
from habitual picking and pulling. There's a stain on my mind.

Against losing I was leaning, praying you'd left behind
at least cigarette smoke. I waited in the dark, bent away like a lone nail
from habitual picking and pulling. There's a stain on my mind.
Your night laughter strung thick in the rafters like a contrail

or at least cigarette smoke. I waited in the dark, bent away like a lone nail.
Pails of night walks, berries in bowls, the hidden door in your throat,
your night laughter strung thick in the rafters like a contrail.
What if you'd ripped a breath hole in my long fleece coat?

Pails of night walks, berries in bowls, the hidden door in your throat,
I know I have dreamt none of it. The house has been empty a long time.
What if I'd ripped a breath hole in my long fleece coat,
if you'd secured a clipboard report of my truest, dearest rinds?

I know I have dreamt none of it. The house has been empty a long time.
Wandering the crown of any tree I was never more glad.
If you'd secured a clipboard report of my truest, dearest rinds
you may have noted my growing lump, my landing pad.

But wandering the crown of any tree I was never more glad,
a long hair in the brine. Soft animal gloves protected my sores.
You may have noted my growing lump. (Admit it, you're sad).
In a stark room I knelt and reeling, felt the wooden floor.

Dust

Our last night together, in the small hours, she took me by the hand
    into the bathroom, ran the water
and soaped me down. Her hands moved over my skin, separately,
    though in concert, like two people
who know each other well but are not lovers, slow-dancing together in
    the bar's farthest corner for the last song

of the evening, that time of night everyone alone dreads. But we were
    not at that moment in a bar—
we were in a Vancouver hotel bathroom, on a warm, late July evening,
    which I admit sounds wonderful
though if I had the night to do over, I might have avoided bathing in
    the small white tiled bathroom

so similar to a Winnipeg hospital room last December, where outside
    the north wind blows the snow
in whatever shapes snow dreams it might be, where from his hospital
    bed my grandfather asks what's new
in the world, looking to the window as if questioning not me but the
    snow swirling past, a man trying

to understand how the cancer comes on, almost imperceptibly, as in,
    One day it's just there in my chest,
as in, *How does it happen, Shane, can you tell me?* And because I have
    no answer for that question,
I respond with another, *What about getting you a shower, Grandpa?*
    And then he turns to me,

and I am slipping his moccasins over the cracked skin of his feet,
     topographical maps bearing the marks
of places he's been: baby shoes in Boston, brown feet on the Red
     River's sandy banks, soft leather
brogues on the cold streets of Sault Ste. Marie. Then I shift his legs,
     spindly after weeks

in bed, and the green cotton gown rides up, revealing the place where
     the clear tube leaves him,
snakes down into the plastic sack, browning with the waste of his
     body. He's so light that with one arm
I lift him, and he pauses, arms hanging over my shoulders, and looks
     around the room with what I imagine

is wonder at the sudden uprightness of the world. And then we are
     walking slowly, in step
with each other, down the hospital corridor, one of his arms over my
     shoulder, the other on the cart
that holds the oxygen canister, and with one hand I steady the cart, in
     the other the bag of piss

swings, and I think of those times during my childhood, grocery
     shopping with my mother,
when she let me push the cart, my hand beside hers on the metal bar,
     how I would concentrate
so hard, that this might be one thing important, one thing to help, as I
     am helping now, moving down

the hallway with my grandfather, and as we pass the open doorways I
     notice he does not look in
exactly, but pauses almost imperceptibly before the large flat
     diamonds of light on the floor,
the harsh light of a prairie winter coming through the windows in
     patients' rooms, and if it is true

that what is captured in the mind remains the same, then perhaps
    what he hesitates over on the polished
gray floors are the prairie winters of his youth. Without asking, I have
    no way of knowing this,
and because I know that for him just moving is tiring enough I am
    silent, my mind returning

to the light of his past as I have held it since tenth grade history class,
    not flat and steady but flickering
black and white in those films from the thirties — the prairie a broad
    dusty tabletop full of ramshackle
cars, jerking across the screen, faces furrowed like the empty field, tire
    marks left in the chaos

of dust. In truth, I watched little else of those films, preferred instead
    to whisper with my friends,
but there was one time when the screen held us all, a close-up of a boy
    our age wearing
flat cap and britches, scowling into the camera — mad as hell to be
    lining up for bread when just last year

his dad's acres spanned whole continents of wheat in his mind. But if
    my grandfather's youth
was that boy I'll never know, for even at this late stage in his life it is
    old-time prairie pride
that prevents him from halting for more than a quick breath at the first
    diamonds of light his skin

has felt in weeks. Pride for the old woman who spends her days
    yelling at the nurses for more
food. Pride for the man who complains loudly the doctors are
    poisoning him. Pride for the woman who calls
out to a family who never comes. If it's for anyone I think it's for these
    people my grandfather's pause

is as slight as a whispered secret, the kind a lover breathes late at night
in a bath, for some reason
you can never know, when her hands take hold of the soft sponge, the
bar of soap, and in the bald light
of the bathroom's too-small tub, she rises up from the water, runs the
sponge along the length

of your arms, leaning into you, so that her breasts swing out close to
your lips and you think
of taking a nipple in your mouth, but giving way instead to some sense
of decorum, decide against it,
and for this, then, or some other reason, she smiles, just as my
grandfather smiles now when

I help him stand in the white tiled shower room, after I've removed
the green gown, and he leans
into me, and the water splashes down, soaking my hair, his hair, my
shirt and his naked body.
And when I pick up the soap and begin, my hands moving slowly
over the places he points to,

I try to imagine the way he might do it, I do not ask how it feels when
I rub the dark bruises made
by daily needles in the crooks of his arms, do not ask because this is
simply a job to be done,
the way those prairie people in the flickering movies of our minds did
the things they had to, silently,

to stay alive. And my hands, graceful in their ignorance, move over his
body, not knowing
this is a rehearsal for something they will witness later, in a Vancouver
hotel room, when the hands
of another person will dance over my body, because this was right
now, and right now the knowledge

my hands carry of how this dance will disappear and return in my life
  is hidden well enough
to keep us both, the old man and me, still moving in my mind, two
  dancers in the smallest hours,
in the farthest corner of a dimly lit bar, our slow turning in one spot a
  kind of contemplation,

of wheat fields, water, snow, skin and dust.

Uganda, 1997

She stands pigeon-toed in too-large
plastic sandals, her Sunday dress
white with orange ruffles, mouth a simple line,
gold studs in tiny ears, close cut hair,
a slight welling in her eyes. Arms motionless
at her sides, she does not hide the stump ends,
the burnt meat's wrinkled dark — where
the soldiers cauterized her wounds.
As they'd been taught, they tried to
make the cuts just above the wrists. But
amphetamines had them shaky; the girl
kept moving her arms. She is eight years old;
the soldiers four years older. They fight
for an army named The Lord's Resistance.
When the cuts are made above the elbow
the soldiers call it "short sleeves."

Mistakes

The nightstick hooks under my armpits.
Don't fucking move, he yells again and yanks.
My chin grinds my chest, knees leave the ground
and then I'm pavement slammed. My mistake is

the cigarette. The way I walk. A smirk.
I should've dropped the smoke the moment flashing
red lights began to re-graffiti that
cinderblock wall. Before the gun led blue-

sleeved arms, face twisted pink, words corkscrewing
the night air: *turn around, hands out slow, I
said slow* — from the car's dark insides.
My mistake is putting out a foot to stub

the cigarette, instead of kneeling right
away. I shouldn't wear these colors. If
I'd just said nothing. I said nothing. I
knelt, hands on head. Rubber gloves gripped my

right wrist, a clink, cold metal, and in two
rough moves he swung my right arm down, my left,
and clink, I was cuffed, and clicking sounds
cut into my wrists. My mistake is walking

the streets at dusk. My mistake is locking
eyes. Should have run. No I shouldn't. He paused.
Behind. His shadow crossed mine then not,
mine then not, in the swinging squad car lights.

Now my ear's pressed to the street. Mashed condom
by my chin. I don't feel anything at first.
Smell tar, dog shit. Then the whole side of my
face burns. My tongue checks for loose teeth. A boot

on my back. Asphalt cold. At eye level:
the other boot, a crushed Coke can. He asks
me what I'm doing here. It's hard to breathe.

The Beach

I always promise Mama I won't go
watch the scrum of green fatigues shove
and stutter-trot the men with soiled
pillow cases over their heads
toward three bullet-pocked palm
trees rooted in a sand clotted red
before the barbed wire wall
vaulted like a little league backstop
as though to keep the wildest pitches
from sailing lost into a crashing border
of jungle trees. I wonder what the thieves
do with what the newspapers tell us
they steal: TVs, gold bracelets,
radios — if they really work for a ring
of wicked *juju* priests, if underneath
their sweaty hoods they hiss chants
and incantations or laugh, knowing
a squadron of flying snakes is right now
blowing down from the north with the hard
Saharan winds to burrow into the navels
of the soldiers' first born sons.
How can men like these be missed
by anyone? On the razor wire perimeter
hiding in a dip of sand I'm belly-down,
roofed by a sheet of junk plywood
sun-shucked to a stone gray. The afternoon
Atlantic picks up, scything into
the shoreline where more green fatigues
lean on scuffed Russian rifles. The hooded

men are bound to the trees. I've heard
the best shooters are brought in especially
for the largest ones, that if you don't hit
them right they're longer to put down.
In front of the three crumpled shapes
a soldier with book open, stops.
Whatever he reads loses itself
in the whipping ocean breeze,
the hoods slack and hanging
like the heavy bells of flowers
with names not yet known to me.

Offering

At the beach, I once saw my father, surrounded by a crowd,
put his lips over the mouth of a man lying on the sand.

There was something in the way he worked: quickly but precisely,
and without flourish. He could have been nailing shingles

or measuring slabs of gyprock for our gray clapboard house
that was leaning into the North Vancouver drizzle long before

we got there. As a child, it always seemed to be raining,
so that years later returning to the city, it feels strange

to be sitting on a woman's bed in a warm square of late
afternoon sun. And perhaps because of the warmth on my skin,

I do not think of when we lived in that rundown house
on the street where the neighbors wrote Nigger Go Home

in jaunty chalk letters stretched to our lane. I do not think
of my mother speaking in the kitchen late at night of our leaving

my father forever silent in what I came to imagine
was the thin music of shame. Why should I? At this moment

a woman is getting ready to step out of the bathroom wearing
nothing but a silk Japanese smoking jacket, and when she does,

she will stand blinking in the bright light, then let her robe fall
away, and in that instant her white skin will shine in the afternoon

light. At this moment, I have not yet placed my hands on her neck,
cradling it, the way my father held the man at the beach, long after

he realized his breath in those dead lungs was helping nothing
and finally, he quit. The man on the beach would never return

to the earth he was born of. And I too have quit, by leaving.
Which is why I cannot tell you, father, of my own encounter

with shame. How brown my hands look on her,
and in their stillness, how useless. This bright offering

I am unable to take, this pale one that lights up the room.

CEILING OF STICKS

San Fernando, Trinidad, 1954

The woman grew up in a village
and did not go to school but her hair
is soft, her skin a good
cinnamon; therefore her indoor sink,
her roof made of tin.

She adds the last canned milk to the glass of Guinness,
scoops the infant up.
The infant drinks.

A dog pack barks
at three boys running behind
three rolling wooden hoops,
saved from toppling over
by a stick's intermittent touch.

The little girl who is my mother
sees them coming, drops
her school dress sewing,
runs back into the kitchen.

She cleans the big cassava-pounding pestle
as her mother adds pigs' feet and more pepper
to the huge pot of simmering green:
crab meat chunks, onions, ham hocks,
hot peppers, okra, dasheen leaves,
hung in a pork fat swamp
thickening into the Sunday callaloo.

The infant crawls among table legs. The fresh-lit
lantern spreads choking kerosene musk.

Soon the father will come home: a short, dark-skinned
man in crisp fedora who brings
a weather, a cloud command:
his wife should feed his sons
as though they are all her own.

Blind Woman of Gondan

Nothing milky, glassy, or wise
about her unlit eyes. With them
she traversed places beyond simile:
coarse gravel plains, desiccated massifs,
denuded rock plateaus, the *hammada*.
With them she walked the desert
heat into the filament that became
her body, as water is allowed by the flower
into the flower's cut stem.

Scattershooting its grit gift
into her deep blue robe
the wind was spun and lost.
But on her hands, feet, face,
it scored and re-scored
a billowing design.

Her forehead bears the molten
architecture: chinked, formal.
The abrasive light-repelling
stain flecks her eyes.
Raised to her depleted lips,
her nails are tiny
demi-planets lifting away
from the sand-pocked fingers,
of one newly exhumed.
The unknown bones of the secret wrist
within the wrist
twist from their dwelling,

making the skin strange. Where does
the coarse cotton robe end
and her creased neck begin?
                              She walked
one month to an empty dispensary.
No screaming, no cursing God:
there is still time to sit in dirt
by the bunkered clinic door,
waiting into the days for a supply plane,
then walking three hundred miles back
to Gondan to learn if
her child has turned
his bare head and died.

Shaving my grandfather in his hospital bed (1)

I plotch foam (crisp
autumn river smell)

on his woolly ear sprigs
scree stubble any

longer it would puncture
my fingers as hanging sunfish

spines he taught me
to grasp another autumn

perched in his canoe
rolling my palm "mouth

to tail" down over
the slick cold gasping things

The Market

The can just misses me. Mama yanks
my arm so hard my shoulder sparks.

We're past rusting grapefruit piled
like slave castle cannon balls,

tan brick soap canyons, red pepper
ravines before I can know, was it

the beggar's throat or his swinging can
that rasped? The morning cooking

fires' soapy haze lifts over open
smoldering gutters, bare-chested men

performing surgery on plastic
lighters. I close my eyes to piss-shit tang,

market mammies wailing prices,
transistor radios' bezerker music: gusting

sermons, flame songs, zigzagged
chatter. Inside the incense woman's

slowed weather Mama stops.
I look up at her midnight

sky hands exchanging
ideograms for *Lemon seller, here?*

and *No, this way, there,* on scraps
of blue air. Off again following

women balancing firewood bundles
on their heads, stepping past silent

paint smear birds flickering
in cages, burning palm oil

cloud-huddles, open-crated
miniature turtles, crab planets

massed in deep buckets, used
shoes slabbed like brown leather

fish. Something's rivuleting the red
ground green. By the lemon alley

Mama drops my hand. I watch
one man stretch a bush rat onto

a bike spoke roasting rack. My arm's
knuckled by something almost cold.

The beggar again, crouching,
can handle looped over smudged wrist.

Leprosy has eaten his hand down to a paw.
He rubs five smooth nubs into my arm.

My People

They washed it
        in the seeping red water
that passes for river.
        The dry season and the place
blistered with a blistered stench.
        Someone smuggled in
a television but the power
        has been erratic since
late July. They cried
        the ceremonial songs,
the sacred crying
        yet the elders' necks
break out in savage rash.
        In the dirt and tent walls, fire.
They painted it the white
        powder of the "place under"
and still a new arrival
        was beaten for his shoes.
They spoke it apologies,
        apologies, praise and apologies.
A distant barking chimes
        the surrounding hills. At least
once an evening, a scream
        spirals the razor wire.
They excused it from the evening
        soccer game. Five men
on strike, playing bone dice
        and marbles day and night.
The fences do not sing

in the wind. They cooked
its favorite meal and did not eat
                          any. Afternoons, a gravel
playing field; sundown, a yard
                          of hard gray eyes
of varied size. People
                          are blind to the taking
of young girls that happens there.
                          They chanted it aloft
in the tent. Some have been
                          there twenty, some all their years.
Young boys trade spent shells
                          for wire tie bands. Telling it
jokes, they held
                          its hands. Mornings mothers
stoop, their straw hand
                          brooms scraping planks.
Strictly no speaking over
                          clothesline borders.
They split the gazelle's
                          belly, caught the cleansing
blood in a petrol can. Babies
                          encrusted from neck down
in twig and dust paste.
                          They thanked it. Small blue
inedible berries under the skeletal
                          shrubs blotching the red clay.
Antlers atop tent peaks. They
                          held its hands, the clans presenting
the holy tins and boxes
                          for inspection. They kissed it
and let it listen to the radio.
                          As there is no rice so there is

dancing no longer. The dogs patrol
                slowly, unswayed by thrown
rocks. The road clean of twigs,
                all firewood guarded
in the homes of three who trade for
                unsingable things. They dried
the gazelle's hide to a flat
                bark. Weekly, nine
or twelve robed ones
                lie down and do not rise.
The last cloud stalled
                overhead in May and was
dismantled by a clanging
                throng. They swept
the stories from around its tent.
                When last did the women
have peppers for a proper stew?
                They scrubbed
the spirit fire stones
                and the cooking fire but
the bile sheen remains. Once
                a boy danced another boy
into a ditch, killing him
                for a rumored tomato. They
begged enough cloth
                and the rope and the oil. A rotted
fish smell would be welcome,
                the shriveled flower
smell is not. All the way up
                the clan tent wall,
chalky trail of footprints.
                They stripped and wound
and wound it in the white cloth.

In the shadows' smallness
of brightest noon, sisters go off
                    searching for boulders. No
more do birds enter this lanky
                    sky. They knotted the cloth
at each end. There are guns
                    and there are no guns
and men with escape plans
                    and plans of boys and women
with wind hitting
                    their shawls. A three
dimensional whale etched into
                    the concrete slab rooting
latrine and pump. They
                    cut the rope in five
and tied off the cloth
                    in five places. Some
names written down:
                    those who built the motor,
those whose freedom came
                    on a stump's underside,
those whose freedom came
                    in a tin can flash flood.
That the ants are aproned
                    and waiting is felt and known
by all. Law is otherwise,
                    a constant twisting silhouette
fired in sun and whims
                    of sand. They have placed it
in the center of the hide.

Shaving my grandfather in his hospital bed (2)

I dip the razor in water
cold as he showed me
In case there's no hot
in the basement bathroom he'd made
where his wife refused to bathe
Like in a war?
because it had no tub he said
Like in a war
because of the moldy dollar
bill smell she said

Cousins read magazines
around pinging machines
You've got the steady hand
He nods at my dad and uncle
against the wall
They're weepers
His twisted mouth
tightens his cheek

His head jerks
hand trailing tubes touching
the bare skin rectangle
He snorts
A respirator sings
His eyes surface
from their pushed-in places
Don't tickle me
I don't bleed
I bring the blade

Stop

Wari cuts the Land Rover engine,
tells his brother Kwesi and I
we're stopping but not staring
and only he's getting out.

Turned too flat against the dirt,
one man's rubber-booted foot
points at the Toyota pickup's mashed
front tire, bent nearly off the rim.
Twin lines of blood track
from the wheel up
and along the hood,
beneath the shoeless foot
of another man wedged headfirst
where there should be windshield.
From arms hung limp out
the driver's window, blood
continues down the shut door,
staining the earth dark.

I'm a pinhole camera.
On the brown grass bank, a man leaning
against a palm tree looks from me to the open
empty suitcase, torn skirt, rusted cutlass,
scattered whiteness that might be rice
scattered on the ground. A man in ripped,
gold-lettered *Disco Duck* shirt smudged with dirt
walks by, doesn't stop.

Wari slams the Rover door,
runs to the closest, who's face up
as though just watching the sky.
I can't see any eyes.

The sun returns. The fan bolted
to the Rover dash slows to nil. I'm sweating.
Can I roll the window down? From the
back seat, Kwesi makes no sound.
Above me on the ceiling, a flash of light:
Wari and another man who's come from
nowhere, moving a wide metal wash basin
from one face lying with his legs
beneath the back end of the truck.

The sun goes away. I'm glass.
I'm stuck in glass and sweating.

Wari and the other man swat
flies. I'm promising I won't look.

Wari kneels, picks up a dented cooking pot,
runs a hand around the truck's gas cap.

If Kwesi's still breathing behind me,
I won't know it. Wari and the other man
shake their heads.
They step away from the truck
and Wari whirls. I swivel back,
a block of uncarved teak.

But I think I've caught what he touched
on the truck body: bulletholes. And
the ground below, a small
round something soft, a clump of rice:
No, it's a child's white sock.

CEILING OF STICKS

To a Curl of Water

1

Corny and adolescent at their age: drinking in a parked car,

spilling onto the cemetery grass, fumbling,
snorting, pulling each other into each other and afterwards lying there

panting among the graves.

Something reduced, unbeautiful in their manner

feels embarrassing
but I can't let you turn from them just yet.

We're waiting for something still far enough away
to be invisible: splitting,

coming together, splitting again,
cruising the cool grass. That is graceful. That is quick.

That is only two white starlight-sheened dogs,

their silent running leaving
a rustling untouched

by the cars rumbling Suffolk street,
untouched even by the lovers' deep breathing

beneath the maple,
and older than the very first Canadian summer.

2

Among Bombay's Parsees, a dog was brought
for dying person and animal to look

into one another's eyes.

The only time I ever studied a dog's eye
was to wash it out with milk.

This was Africa:
our dog, exploring the yard's back corner,

hit with cobra spit.

When I arrived the dog listed in a nowhere-going shuffle,
the V-headed snake waited, coiled. I threw

a stick, picked the dog up, its eye already phlegmy,
static. Back then Ghana

didn't have television. We made do with power cuts,

attempted coups. Today two Canadian night dogs
are enough, mouths open

but not panting though they run hard

as if bringing another world's news.

3

Some ancient peoples will kill a white dog
and after the feasting, songs, dancing,

mumbled prayer ends the ritual, a whispering
like something moving through grass,

and what else can this animal bring the next world

but a hushed sound that comes from the beginning

of not being — not being, and then being gone?
A sound mixing with an Atlantic Ocean smell

and the seashell mortar wall smell

moldy slave dungeons hold
in those abandoned British castles

still pinning West Africa's coast
centuries after the final slave has been led out

to the last ship,

and around the castles' thick white-washed walls
that sound hardening. Ghana International School's

assembly hall: tin-roofed, unwalled, where we stood,
boy blue pants white shirts,

girl green white striped dresses,
the headmistress each morning leading us singing

God Save the Queen and now just a lizard
tasting the paw-paw tree's shade.

A loudness, then a trailing away I can't forget.
A curl of water growing inside me,

and the after-wave's unraveling hiss.

Kumasi, Labadi, Nima, Accra: Ghanaian cities
and slum cities within those cities and beaches

littered with plastic bags and graying palm fronds.

Wawa, Fort Frances, Lively, Rainy River:
small Ontario highway towns

nearly hidden from legions of swooshing truck tires
by pine tree forest walls and piled granite.

Snow dissolving in melted snow.

4

This world's companions, the next world's guides,
slaloming the tombstoned woods near Suffolk Street:

twin dogs, do you move as the mind moves
or a mind's final two thoughts move

as the eyes ice-over?

At the end that is not really an end
you lead us to the shallow dugout canoe

and down the river
into another story.

You run the big Volta Road house
back patio where the American

diplomat girl lived: blue bikini, silver anklet,

pale freckled skin, blonde ponytailed hair.

And this is a story
without grand meanings, whose fulcrum

is just a motion itself: being to being gone,

the dry season's Harmattan wind, red dust
powdering a vacant home's bare floors, air rushing

in a louvered window wall
out an opposite windowed wall

the scent of snake's venom,
the after-wave's unraveling hiss.

And leaving the school assembly hall
the American girl

pointing to a group of us, laughing and saying "y'all,"

as she motioned with her hand,

those shiny red fingernails all it took
for us to skip school

and drink beer at her place. That afternoon

she barbecued something, wore heels with her bikini,
but what I most recall was her walking

the pool deck with a bag of miraculous Twinkies.

Back then in Ghana you couldn't buy
a stick of gum, let alone dessert.

In Ghana at that time our desires were as modest
as the story I'm going to tell you now:

late one August night in Ontario
a woman and I cracked open beers and smoked

cigarettes in a parked car and soon were kissing, fumbling,
opening a door and falling onto the grass,

the night air thick with the day's humidity,

the evening's dew already down. She

stood a moment —
her calves, I remember,

glistening — acres of tombstones tracking
the hill's slow rise beyond us.

Taking my hand, she led me to a maple,

we kissed there a long time,
then stripped off our clothes and made love

and afterwards quietly lay in the yellowing light.

The week we'd known each other we'd done little
else. It was wonderful

and continuing that way. An insect bit

my neck. I sat up, felt another on my ankle,
more behind my knee.

Where my back had been, an anthill . . .

Out of nowhere they came:
two white dogs we did not hear

so much as feel,
their fur brushing our skin, the woman crying out,

the two dogs sniffing us
and before I could get to my feet, gone —

two white shapes weaving away through
the gravestones. We smiled at each other

and she nodded and touched my arm.

I don't know exactly when it happened.
The next year something jarred

loose: even together
we were always slightly angled away. Later

she moved to a city and I did not follow her
and we did not discuss why.

Perhaps that night
in the cemetery a final hush fell upon us —

You, irrevocable, you, the song's refrain
might have been —

the lust engulfing us
was not the fire we thought

was nothing more
than the receding notion of water

after a surge of water.

5

Later in the American girl's story,
her teenaged guests must leave

her party and die in a fireball car crash,

or the hostess, terribly drunk, should drown
in the pool. In reality that evening

Ghana's only newspaper front-paged
her father's photo above an article accusing

him of being a CIA agent.

Next morning's roll call
our teacher Mrs. Danquah skipped

the girl's name. Noon
I snuck off, walked the two miles:

her gate hung open, house windows
dark and unshining,

rooms empty, pool deck chairs gone.

Calm as that tropical afternoon, the clear, still
pool water gave nothing away.

No adult spoke of her family again.
It was as though I'd imagined her.

....

A person is here a moment and then Nothing

takes her seat in class. That is the motion described
yet it does not describe the motion. Somewhere

in there a swinging, a movement I hope to see —

the missing, the lost, the dead, the hidden, the invisible,

and the white dogs leading them all — to see it
and fall in behind them one day. Two dogs

sprinting ahead, circling back, making sure
we're still coming, two dogs running the patio

where the bikinied girl sits laughing and saying "y'all."

She who turns to watch them and in that turning becomes
a soft question mark cased in bone.

6

Some people say what we are is representation
and that representation is a lie.

But someone touches your arm and you shiver,

snow dissolves in melted snow and both *were*
once there. Something happens and something else

happens, unending, I am guessing. We are made

of relations, I am guessing, the tractor-trailer's airbrakes

singe the wind and the wind feels softened, I am saying.

Even now, starlight and the street lamp's glow
fall together into the maple's leaves

and are staggered by the maple's leaves,
yellowing the grass, gravestones and . . .

Once in a small town without gravestones, grass,
street lamps, maples, the first man I saw

climbed into my car and in French
directed me to a government guesthouse —

because he explained, in this part of Mali
there were no motels, because the town

had not seen a visitor in thirty years.

A dog brushes against you, ants carry
away the eye of a dead sparrow,

a car disappears down a moon crater pothole,
and reappears on the other side.

A fact dislodges and joins history and we happen.

Placing the kerosene lantern on the floor, the man
softly shut the door behind him,

leaving me sitting on the bare torn mattress.

In the windowless room, the lantern flame

hissed to a blow torch roar. I pulled
the ceiling fan's motionless string

and the blades did not turn. I waved my hand

before my face and the air that moved
was no cooler than the air around it

and so felt like nothing, a nothing that moved:
frighteningly final and blessed

with a lizard's linear directness —
orange flash — darting at its prey.

Out in the courtyard, the smiling

guesthouse proprietor presented a menu
and each time I pointed to an item he told me

in extremely polite French, the item did not exist.

7

I still believe in small Ontario towns. I believe
in aging maples, the Sub-Saharan night sky, spitting

snakes, dirty beaches. I believe in tractor-trailers,
the endless fact of a wave's story, the green sea mold

growing in slave castle walls. I believe

a girl and her family cannot disappear.

8

The guesthouse proprietor brought
a meat dish bathed in thick red sauce.

Scraped off, it left a fatless gray mass.
I sawed into it and chewed and when I was done

the proprietor asked how I liked it

and I said I liked it, which was only a partial lie.

I thought you didn't have any lamb, I said

and he said, *It was not lamb, it was dog.*
Bending down, he held his hand

inches from the ground.

Small dog, he said, *Very sweet.*

9

Tell me to go and I'll never leave, the song's
refrain might have been. And hold me again, she says,

just hold me, the feeling of her voice
like a whistling along a dark street,

and the white dogs veer off,

a widening sound

filling the empty eye sockets

of sparrows, filling the faded plastic pails
and shovels children leave on beaches,

filling the broad open leaves of palms.

To order or obtain more information on these or other University of Nebraska Press titles, visit www.nebraskapress.unl.edu.

The poem "Dust" has been adapted
into a film. For more information
please visit www.shanebook.com.